Intro to French

Bela Davis

Français

Abdo Kids Junior
is an Imprint of Abdo Kids
abdobooks.com

Abdo
INTRO TO LANGUAGE
Kids

abdobooks.com

Published by Abdo Kids, a division of ABDO, P.O. Box 398166, Minneapolis, Minnesota 55439.

Abdo Kids Junior™ is a trademark and logo of Abdo Kids.

Printed in China

102023

012024

Consultant: Harriet Abdo

Photo Credits: Getty Images, Shutterstock

Production Contributors: Teddy Borth, Jennie Forsberg, Grace Hansen

Design Contributors: Candice Keimig, Colleen McLaren

Library of Congress Control Number: 2023937680

Publisher's Cataloging-in-Publication Data

Names: Davis, Bela, author.

Title: Intro to French / by Bela Davis

Description: Minneapolis, Minnesota : Abdo Kids, 2024 | Series: Intro to language | Includes online resources and index.

Identifiers: ISBN 9781098268299 (lib. bdg.) | ISBN 9781098268992 (ebook) | ISBN 9781098269340 (Read-to-Me ebook)

Subjects: LCSH: French language--Juvenile literature. | Informal language learning--Juvenile literature. | Language and languages--Juvenile literature. | Bilingual books--Juvenile literature.

Classification: DDC 418.00--dc23

Table of Contents

Intro to French

French is spoken around the world. Let's learn some words!

French	bienvenue
(sound guide)	(bee•en•venew)
English	welcome

N
W
E
S
Europe
France
Africa
South America
French is an official language

un
(uh)
one

deux
(deu)
two

six
(sees)
six

sept
(set)
seven

trois
(trh•wa)
three

quatre
(kat•rh)
four

cinq
(sahnk)
five

huit
(weet)
eight

neuf
(neuhf)
nine

dix
(dees)
ten

onze
(onz)
eleven

douze
(dooz)
twelve

seize
(sez)
sixteen

dix-sept
(dee•set)
seventeen

13
treize
(trez)
thirteen

14
quatorze
(katorz)
fourteen

15
quinze
(kanz)
fifteen

18
dix-huit
(dees•weet)
eighteen

19
dix-neuf
(dees•neuhf)
nineteen

20
vingt
(van)
twenty

violet
(vee•o•leh)
purple
bleu
(bleuh)
blue
blanc
(blauhn)
white
jaune
(dsh•oh•n)
yellow

orange
(o•rh•auhn•dsh)
orange
vert
(ve•hr)
green
rouge
(rh•ouh•dsh)
red
noir
(nwa•rh)
black
les couleurs
(cooler)
the colors

bonjour
(bon•jshur)
hello

au revoir
(o•ruh•vwar)
goodbye

salut
(sa•lu)
hi/bye

bonne nuit
(bohn•nwee)
good night

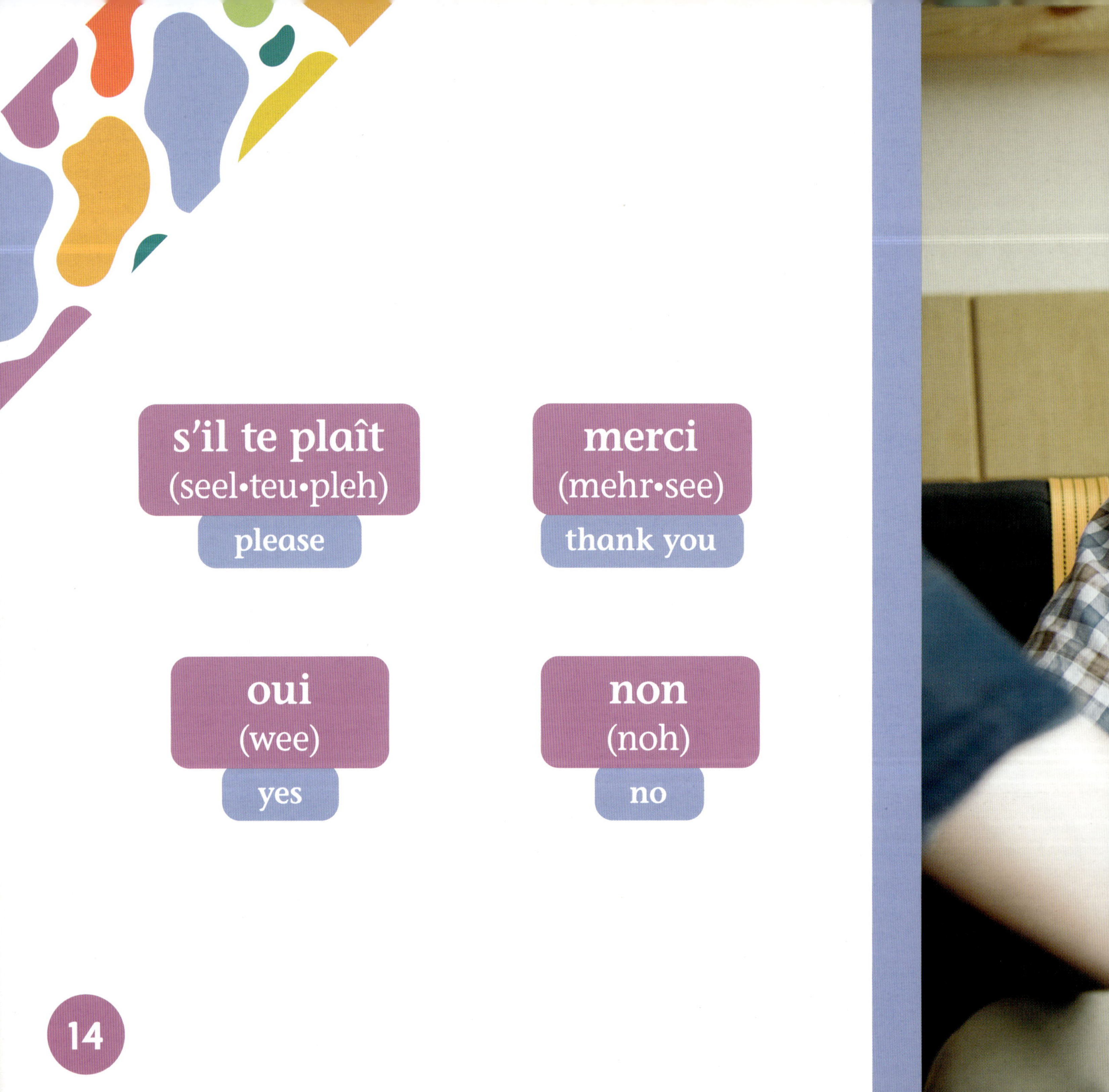

s'il te plaît
(seel•teu•pleh)
please

merci
(mehr•see)
thank you

oui
(wee)
yes

non
(noh)
no

ma famille
(fa•miy)
my family

ma maman
(meh•mohn)
my mom

mon papa
(pa•pa)
my dad

ma sœur
(seur)
my sister

mon frère
(frer)
my brother

ma grand-mère
(grand mehr)
my grandmother

mon grand-père
(grand pehr)
my grandfather

ma tante
(tant)
my aunt

mon oncle
(on•kl)
my uncle

le chat
(sha)
cat
les animaux
(a•ni•mo)
the animals
le chien
(she•in)
dog

le poisson
(pwa•sohn)
fish
l'oiseau
(wa•zoo)
bird

Lieux – Places

la maison
(me•zon)

house

l'école
(ee•col)

school

le parc
(pahrk)

park

la plage
(plaj)

beach

L'alphabet – The Alphabet

letter	A	B	C	D	E	F
sound	ah	bay	say	day	euh	ef

G	H	I	J	K	L
jhay	ash	ee	ghee	kah	el

M	N	O	P	Q	R
em	en	oh	pay	ku	air

S	T	U	V	W	X
ess	tay	ooh	vay	doubleh vay	eeks

Y	Z
ee·greck	zed

Index